V *for* Vanishing

An Alphabet of Endangered Animals

Patricia Mullins

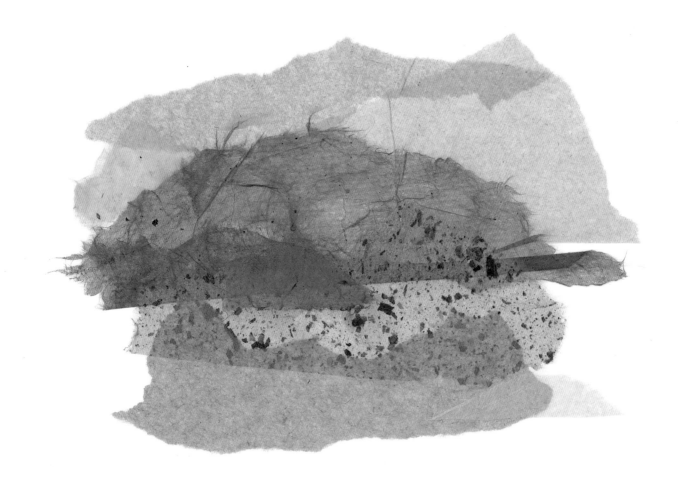

HarperCollins*Publishers*

We share this planet with a rich diversity of animal and plant species. Humans, though, have become so abundant that they now dominate, threatening the survival of other species. While extinction is a natural process, the loss of most species during the past five hundred years can be directly attributed to the rapid expansion of the human population. The twentieth century has seen an enormous number of plant and animal species threatened with extinction as humans continue to make excessive demands on the environment and blatantly destroy vital parts of it.

It is essential that we all be made aware of and understand what this destruction means, not only to individual species but to the careful balance of ecosystems and ultimately to the existence of human beings. Only through awareness and international cooperation between governments and people can this crisis be averted. For despite protective laws and much publicity, some endangered animals are still being poached. These include the Mountain Gorilla, the Rhinoceroses of Asia and Africa, Macaws, African and Asian Elephants, the Snow Leopard, the Yak, and the Queen Alexandra Birdwing (the largest known butterfly in the world). The Humpback Whale is only one of a number of whale species that are endangered or vulnerable, and despite this, whaling remains a contentious issue among nations. Logging continues in forests that provide homes for the Sloth, Orangutan, Cape Mountain Zebra, Jaguar, Uakari, and Gastric Brooding Frog, while the habitats of the Quoll, Numbat, Fairy Armadillos, Indus River Dolphin, Fijian Crested Iguana, and Latifis Viper are still being developed for human purposes.

Zoos and organizations committed to the survival of species have developed captive breeding programs that aim to breed some of those that face certain extinction if left in their natural environments. If breeding is successful, the animals are returned to their original habitats in the hope that the species will reestablish themselves. Species that seem to have been successfully bred under these programs include the Przewalski's Horse, California Condor, and Mauritius Kestrel. Efforts to breed the Giant Panda continue in several countries, particularly China.

The animals in this book are all at risk of becoming extinct in the near future if they and their habitats are not nurtured. It is my hope that by highlighting the plight of these beautiful and fascinating creatures, this book will encourage a love for the animals and plants of our world, and the desire to care for all of them.

Patricia Mullins
Melbourne, 1993

Aa Armadillo

Pink Fairy Armadillo
Chlamyphorus truncatus
Argentina

Bb Butterfly

Queen Alexandra's Birdwing
Ornithoptera alexandris
Papua New Guinea

Cc Condor

California Condor
Gymnogyps californianus
United States of America

Dd Dolphin

Indus River Dolphin
Platanista indi
Pakistan

Ee Elephant

Asian Elephant
Elephas maximus
Asia

Ff

Frog

Gastric Brooding Frog
Rheobatrachus silus
Australia

Gg Gorilla

Mountain Gorilla
Gorilla gorilla beringei
Africa

Hh Horse

Przewalski's Horse
Equus przewalskii
Mongolia

Ii

Iguana

Fijian Crested Iguana
Brachylophus vitiensis
Fiji

J j Jaguar

Jaguar
Panthera onca
South America

Kk Kestrel

Mauritius Kestrel
Falco punctatus
Mauritius

Ll Leopard

Snow Leopard
Panthera uncia
Central Asia

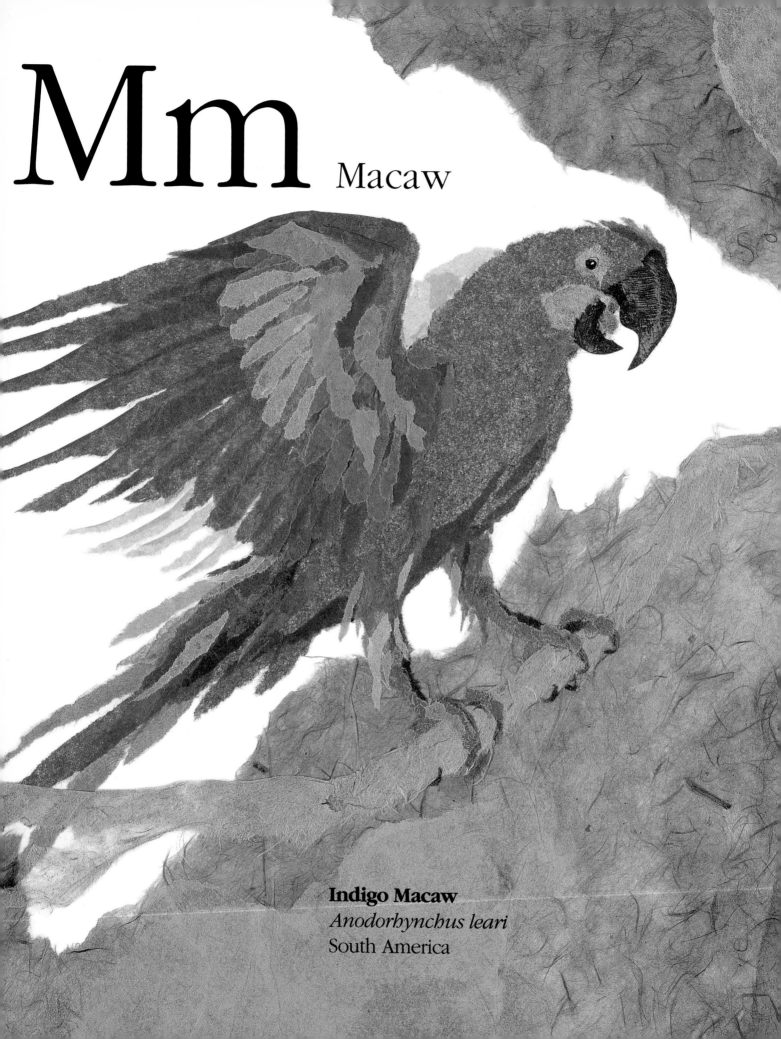

Mm Macaw

Indigo Macaw
Anodorhynchus leari
South America

Nn Numbat

Numbat
Myrmecobius fasciatus
Australia

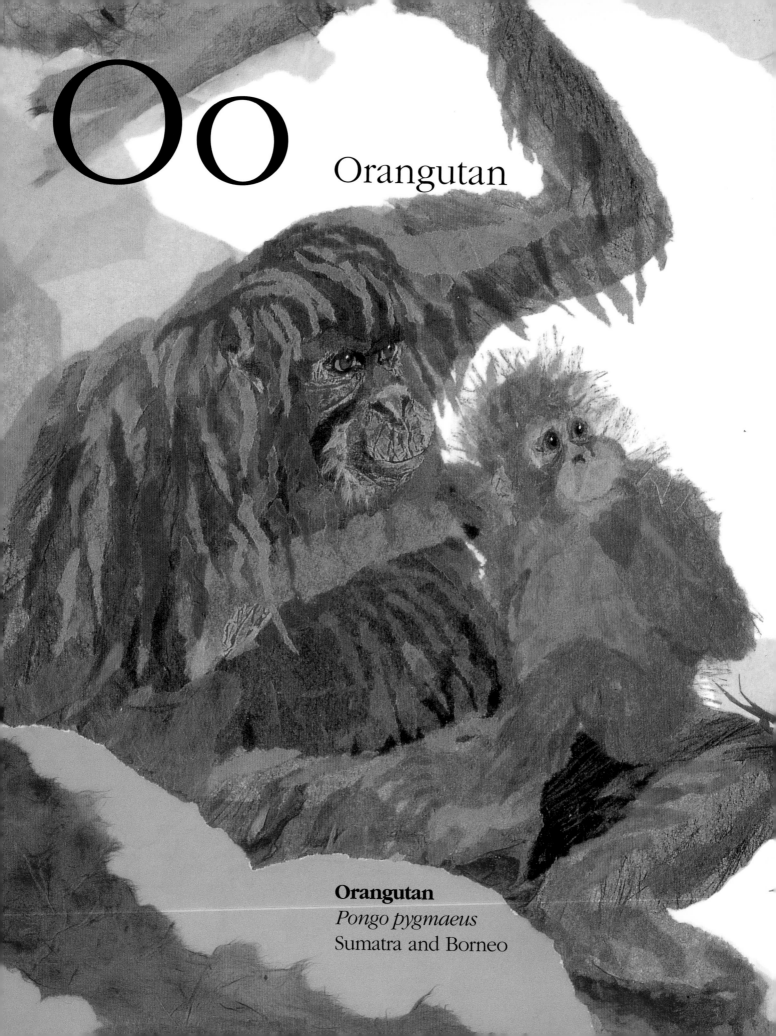

Oo Orangutan

Orangutan
Pongo pygmaeus
Sumatra and Borneo

Pp Panda

Giant Panda
Ailuropoda melanoleuca
China

Qq Quoll

Western Quoll
Dasyurus geoffroii
Australia

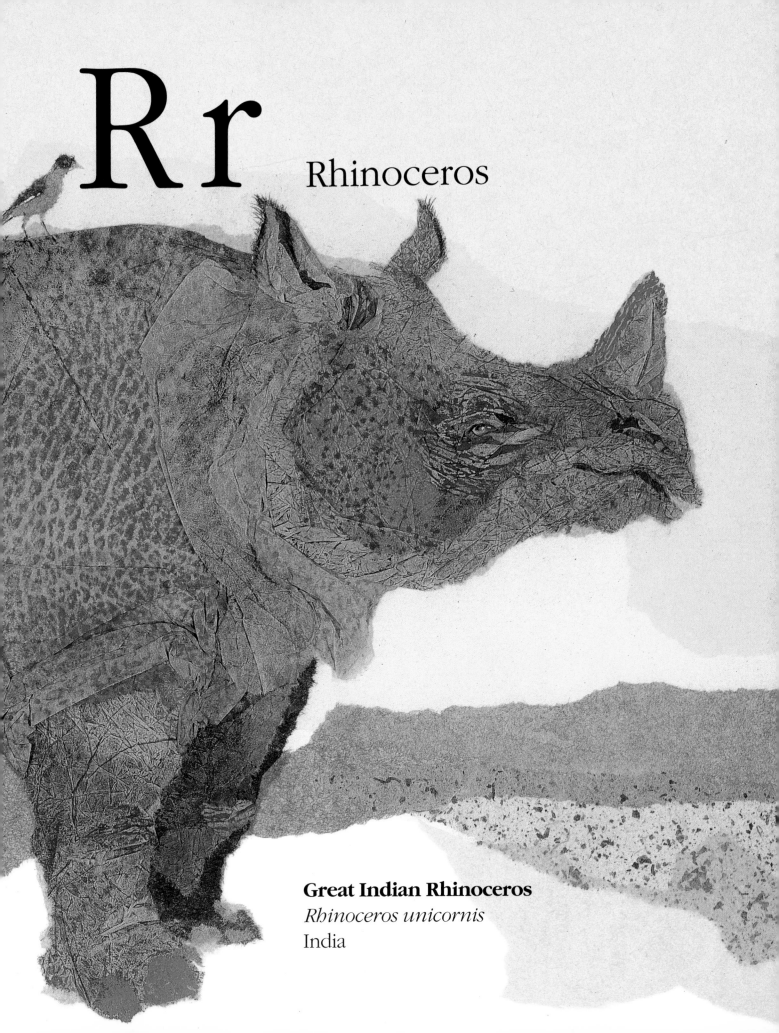

Rr Rhinoceros

Great Indian Rhinoceros
Rhinoceros unicornis
India

S s Sloth

Maned Sloth
Bradypus torquatus
South America

Tt Tortoise

Galapagos Tortoise
Geochelone elephantopus
Galapagos Islands

Uu Uakari

Red Uakari
Cacajao calvus
South America

Vv Viper

Latifis Viper
Vipera latifii
Iran

Ww Whale

Humpback Whale
Megaptera novaeangliae
All major oceans

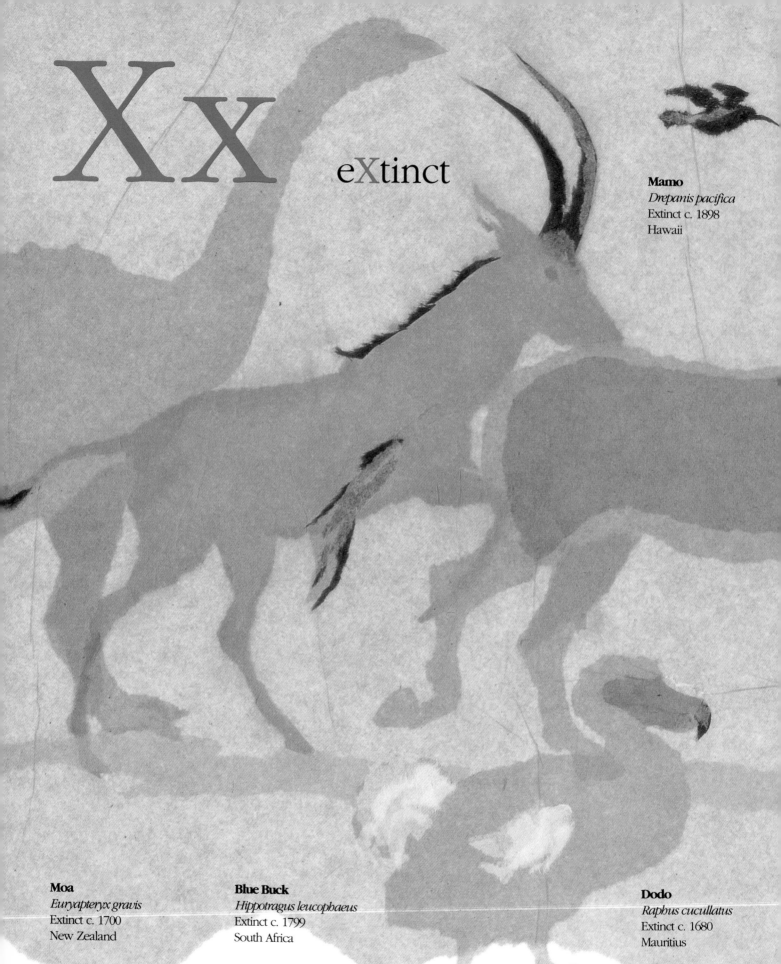

Xx eXtinct

Mamo
Drepanis pacifica
Extinct c. 1898
Hawaii

Moa
Euryapteryx gravis
Extinct c. 1700
New Zealand

Blue Buck
Hippotragus leucophaeus
Extinct c. 1799
South Africa

Dodo
Raphus cucullatus
Extinct c. 1680
Mauritius

Pink Headed Duck
Rhodonessa caryophyllacca
Extinct c. 1924
India

Passenger Pigeon
Ectopistes migratorius
Extinct c. 1914
United States of America

Quagga
Equus burchelli quagga
Extinct c. 1883
South Africa

Atlas Bear
Ursus arctos crowtheri
Extinct c. 1870
North Africa

Newfoundland White Wolf
Canis lupus beothulus
Extinct c. 1911
Newfoundland

Thylacine
Thylacimus cynocephalus
Extinct c. 1936
Australia

Yy Yak

Yak
Bos grunniens
Central Asia

Zz Zebra

Cape Mountain Zebra
Equus zebra zebra
South Africa

For my husband, John, and my son, Hamish

ACKNOWLEDGMENTS

My thanks to the following individuals and organizations:

Dr. Claes Andrén, Dept. of Zoology, University of Göteborg, Göteborg, Sweden, for information on the Latifis Viper;

Prof. Mike Tyler, Dept. of Zoology, University of Adelaide, Adelaide, Australia, for information on the Gastric Brooding Frog;

Dept. of Entomology, National Museum of Victoria, Australia, for information on the Queen Alexandra Birdwing;

IUCN, The World Conservation Union, Gland, Switzerland;

World Wide Fund for Nature International, Gland, Switzerland;

World Wildlife Fund, Washington, DC, USA;

Judye and Richard Thompson, Melbourne, Australia.

And also to the animals of the Royal Melbourne Zoological Gardens, who are a continual source of inspiration and information. In particular, for this book, the Jaguar, Snow Leopards, Asian Elephants, and Orangutans. The Lowland Gorillas, Chapman's Zebras, Blue and Yellow Macaws, and Aldabra Giant Tortoises provided further inspiration.

With special thanks from the Publisher and Patricia Mullins to Chris Cheng, Education Officer, Taronga Zoo, Sydney, Australia.

SOURCES

Convention on International Trade in Endangered Species of Wild Fauna & Flora (CITES). Annual publication of the Federal Wildlife Permit Office of the US Fish & Wildlife Service.
Red List of Threatened Animals. Cambridge: International Union for Conservation of Nature and Natural Resources (IUCN), 1988.
Endangered and Threatened Wildlife and Plants. US Dept. of the Interior, US Fish & Wildlife Service, 1992.
Walker, Ernest P. *Mammals of the World.* 5th ed. Baltimore, MD: Johns Hopkins Press, 1992.
Day, David. *The Encyclopedia of Vanished Species.* Rev. ed. London: Universal Books, 1989.
Flannery, T., P. Kendall, & K. Wynn-Moylan. *Australia's Vanishing Mammals: Endangered and Extinct Native Species.* Sydney: Reader's Digest, 1990.

Illustrative technique: The animals in this book have been interpreted completely in collage using a variety of tissue papers and, occasionally, Ostrich feathers. Paint and crayon have been used sparingly for minor detailing and surface textures.

The paper used for the pages in this book is from plantation-grown timber. The endpapers are natural recycled paper, and the case boards are also recycled.

V for Vanishing
An Alphabet of Endangered Animals
Copyright © 1993 by Patricia Mullins
First published in 1993 by Margaret Hamilton Books Pty Ltd, Australia.
Printed in Hong Kong. All rights reserved.
Library of Congress Cataloging-in-Publication Date
Mullins, Patricia, 1952-
V for vanishing : an alphabet of endangered animals / Patricia Mullins.
p.   cm.
Summary: An ABC book featuring illustrations of endangered and extinct animals from around the world.
ISBN 0-06-023556-X. — ISBN 0-06-023557-8 (lib. bdg.) — ISBN 0-06-443471-0 (pbk.)
1. Endangered species—Juvenile literature. 2. English language—Alphabet—Juvenile literature. [1. Rare animals. 2. Alphabet.] I. Title.
QL83.M84   1994   93-8181
591.52'9—dc20   CIP
AC
First Harper Trophy edition, 1997